VOWEL ADVENTURES

UMA AND THE RUMBLING TRUCKS

AN ADVENTURE WITH THE VOWEL U

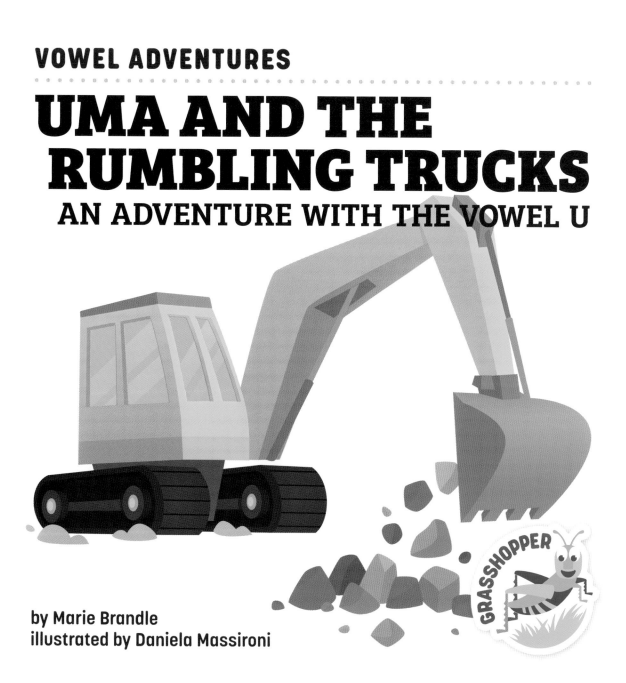

by Marie Brandle
illustrated by Daniela Massironi

GRASSHOPPER

Tools for Parents & Teachers

Grasshopper Books enhance imagination and introduce the earliest readers to fiction with fun storylines and illustrations. The easy-to-read text supports early reading experiences with repetitive sentence patterns and sight words.

Before Reading

- Look at the cover illustration. What do readers see? What do they think the book will be about?

- Look at the picture glossary together. Sound out the words. Ask readers to identify the first letter of each vocabulary word.

Read the Book

- "Walk" through the book, reading to or along with the reader. Point to the illustrations as you read.

After Reading

- Review the picture glossary again. Ask readers to locate the words in the text.

- Ask the reader: What does a short 'u' sound like? What does a long 'u' sound like? Which words did you see in the book with these sounds? What other words do you know that have these sounds?

Grasshopper Books are published by Jump!
5357 Penn Avenue South
Minneapolis, MN 55419
www.jumplibrary.com

Library of Congress Cataloging-in-Publication Data

Names: Brandle, Marie, 1989– author.
Massironi, Daniela, illustrator.
Title: Uma and the rumbling trucks: an adventure with the vowel u / by Marie Brandle; illustrated by Daniela Massironi.
Description: Minneapolis, MN: Jump!, Inc., [2022]
Series: Vowel adventures
Includes reading tips and supplementary back matter.
Audience: Ages 5-7.
Identifiers: LCCN 2021002195 (print)
LCCN 2021002196 (ebook)
ISBN 9781636902494 (hardcover)
ISBN 9781636902500 (paperback)
ISBN 9781636902517 (ebook)
Subjects: LCSH: Readers (Primary)
Trucks–Juvenile fiction.
Classification: LCC PE1119.2 .B738 2022 (print)
LCC PE1119.2 (ebook)
DDC 428.6/2–dc23
LC record available at https://lccn.loc.gov/2021002195
LC ebook record available at https://lccn.loc.gov/2021002196

Editor: Eliza Leahy
Direction and Layout: Anna Peterson
Illustrator: Daniela Massironi

Printed in the United States of America at Corporate Graphics in North Mankato, Minnesota.

Table of Contents

Trucks Rule!

It is a sunny summer day.

"I could use some fun," Uma mumbles.

All of a sudden . . .

Thump! Bump! Thud!

Uma jumps up. She runs to the curb.

"Trucks!" Uma shouts.
"I am nuts about trucks!"

Trucks rumble.

They lug supplies.

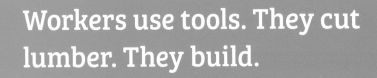

Workers use tools. They cut lumber. They build.

Uma studies the trucks.

"That must be fun!" she says.

A bulldozer pushes mud.

"Trucks rule!" Uma says.

A dump truck is full.
It lugs rubble.

"Uh-oh! A huge puddle!"
Uma shouts.

Mud flies!

A forklift picks stuff up.
It puts stuff down. *Clunk!*

"Such a ruckus!" Uma says.

Uma salutes the driver.
"Keep it up!" she says.

He gives a thumbs-up.

Let's Review Vowel U!

Point to the words with the short 'u' sound you saw in the book.
Point to the words with the long 'u' sound.

huge   **cut**   **puddle**   **jumps**   **pushes**   **use**

Picture Glossary

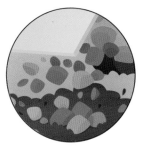

rubble
Broken pieces of stone, brick, and concrete left behind when a building is taken down.

ruckus
A noisy situation.

rumble
To move with a low, deep, continuous noise like the sound of thunder.

salutes
Shows respect by raising a hand to one's forehead.